Coercive Control: Breaking Free From Psychological Abuse

CW00552030

30127 08878075 9

While every precaution has been taken in the preparation of this book, the publisher assumes no responsibility for errors or omissions, or for damages resulting from the use of the information contained herein.

COERCIVE CONTROL: BREAKING FREE FROM PSYCHOLOGICAL ABUSE

First edition. April 20, 2020.

Copyright © 2020 Lauren Kozlowski.

ISBN: 978-1393659327

Written by Lauren Kozlowski.

Table of Contents

By

Lauren Kozlowski

For those who are enduring, or have endured, the systematic torture of being isolated, threatened and deprived of your freedom.

Chapter One Introduction: What is Coercive Control in a Relationship?

Abuse isn't always physical. A controlling spouse is often viewed as the one who lashes out at their partner, who uses violence to get them to behave in a certain way. People tend to use words like 'aggressive', and 'violent' to describe their thoughts on what they think a controlling spouse is. Whilst these opinions can often be true, the opposite is commonplace, too; a controlling relationship where there is no physical abuse. Or, a controlling relationship where the abuse is *rarely* physical. What would you call this abuse, though. Emotional abuse? Mental abuse? Abuse by emotional control? Control through fear?

For a long time, the term 'coercive control' wasn't really a 'thing'; it existed, but it wasn't used to describe, so accurately, the kind of abuse that affects millions of us every day. It sums up the acts and patterns of vile threats, crippling humiliation and frightening intimidation so many of us have to endure every single day from our partner. Coercive control sees the victim be systematically punished, with fear being the reins that control their actions. The abuser in this type of relationship seeks to harm, chastise, and frighten their victim into submission, enabling them to have complete control over their subdued partner. For so many of us, we can't comprehend the reason why someone would want this. As someone who has been through years of systematic abuse like this, I sometimes thought to myself 'I'd never be able to treat anybody the way you treat me, let alone someone I loved.' I couldn't get to grips with why someone would treat their partner so despicably yet purport to love them. The dissonance in what I was being told to what was really happening only served to push me closer to my abuser; I was so confused and full of self-doubt that I believed his words.

his controlling behavior is to ensure the victim is dependent on eir abuser. This happens when the abuser isolates their victim from pport, exploiting them, stripping them of their independence and gulating their day-to-day behavior. This was my life for many years, here I was deprived of the comfort of family and friends, where y money was taken from me, my movements were tracked and onitored, and my entire being was simply the ghost of the person I ed to be before the abuse. I lived in a rigid state of constant fear and t-churning anxiety, worried about the next spate of abuse I would ve to endure. I lived a life where all of my words, actions, and even oughts served only to pacify my abuser.

ow I'm free of my abuser, and I want to make sure that everyone derstands just what makes up this evil, all-consuming, entirely ntrolling type of abuse. Too many times I've heard people reach t to me to speak to me about the controlling relationship they're , but then end up sticking up for their abuser by saying, 'But they n't hit me, so maybe I'm being silly,' or 'They've only been gressive a couple of times, and I suppose that they just have a ntrolling personality type.' I understand the rationale behind this, defend your abuser because it helps avoid the horrible emotions having to confront that you're in an abusive partnership, but this ly serves to keep you in the controlling relationship. People will essage me on social media, and I'm always happy to give my advice, oughts, and opinions when someone offers up their story or asks a question. However, one of the reasons I wanted to pen this ok was because of the vast amount of people who reach out to and then recoil when I suggest they're enduring coercive control. m going through this myself, to the hours upon hours of research e done on the topic thereafter, to the dozens of real-life stories

that land in my inbox every day, I feel like this power-fuelled typ
of relationship is on the rise. I checked the stats online and
corroborated what I was thinking - cases of coercive control ha
doubled in the last year (and that's just the ones that get reported
police - I imagine the true figure is much, much higher than the o
you'll get from a quick Google search).

I want this book to serve as a tool of sorts for those who are in
controlling relationship like this. I also want it to help expose th
(often hidden) form of abuse and for it to affirm to the masses th
coercive control is not only real, but it's often closer to home tha
you think. I want this to guide victims of this type of abuse towar
a place of understanding it, which enables them to tackle it with
much more resolve.

So, to summarize this complicated, cruel form of abuse into
sentence, I'd have to say coercive control is a set of invisible chai
that tethers the victim to their abuser. It's a sense of fear that satura
all elements of the victim's life. It works by limiting their hum
rights by stripping them of their liberty which reduces their abili
to take action. The victim becomes captive in an almost fictionaliz
unreal world that the abuser creates. Once engulfed in this w
of fiction, the victim is entrapped in a world of contradictio
confusion, and prevalent fear.

Chapter Two The Signs of Coercive Control: Heed These Red Flags

———

"Poisonous relationships can alter our perception. You can spend years thinking you're worthless, when in reality, you're chronically underappreciated"

Coercive control creeps up on you slowly. You don't enter the relationship and see your spouse immediately begin to restrict your freedom or get ragefully mad when you see your family. It rarely happens as boldly as that. More often than not, the coercive control seeps into the relationship bit by bit, until you find yourself in the pits of the abuse, wading through it daily, unable to find a way out.

Before the abuse takes full force and grips you entirely, there are usually red flags. My first red flag was when I went to see my mother who was only twenty minutes away from my ex's home. I told him I'd be an hour, but ended up being nearly two. When I arrived back home, he wouldn't speak to me. I would get one word answers, and when I asked what was up, I'd get a cold answer of, 'Nothing.' This lasted the whole day and part way into the next day, and I was still none the wiser as to what I'd done wrong. Surely, I thought, it couldn't be because I was a little later than I anticipated coming back from my mother's? It was on his terms when he decided to speak to me again, and he wouldn't explain the silent treatment he gave me. After this little episode passed, a few days later I mentioned I was going to see my mother, to which he replied, 'Are you going to lie about how long you'll be this time?,' which only reaffirmed to me why he was so mad at me previously - because I took too long visiting my mother. I was taken aback, and didn't know how to answer this. I thought I must have really hurt him, and knowing he had a rough time with his ex that caused him trust issues (which is a narcissistic line if I've ever heard one right there), I decided I'd make sure I was home on time this time.

And so began years of abusive, coercive control that only escalated from that point onwards.

Red flags will pop up throughout the beginning stages of the relationship, and the ones I'll outline below were all prevalent in my relationship. Did I know they were red flags at the time? Yes, they did alarm me, but as someone who is incredibly trusting, empathetic, and gave the benefit of the doubt, I didn't see them as the red flags they were. These warnings were just obstacles to overcome in the relationship at the time, and I thought I could make my partner better - that I could fix his trust issues, that his jealousy was because he didn't want to lose me. Of course, these thoughts were heavily fogged over with the manipulative gaslighting I was exposed to in this relationship, too, and hindsight is a wonderfully painful thing when you see just how controlled you were.

The red flags that present themselves to warn you of a dangerously controlling, abusive partner are generally very similar in each circumstance. You may find a lot of the following red flags have popped up in your situation, if not all of them. These warnings are things I've experienced personally, as well as other victims who've been through the turmoil of a controlling relationship.

Flag #1. Isolation from your support system.

A controlling partner will try their mightiest to cut you off from your friends and family or at the very least, limit your contact with them so you can't so easily receive the support you need. Even if you're close with your family and have a close-knit group of friends, a controlling spouse *will* find ways to separate you from them. Their inner jealousy and need for control somehow finds a way to beat you down every time. There are a few ways they do this:

● They might suggest a shared phone and social media accounts for 'ease' or 'convenience'. This would mean deleting your own social media profiles and setting up a joint account. Alarm bells go off in my head now when I see couples who share social media. A Facebook profile with both of their names screams controlling to me - 'John & Jane Smith' type profiles have red flags waving for me. Of course, in some cases this may be entirely innocent, and older couples particularly tend to share one phone for ease. But, in my experience, those shared profiles are a window into a toxic relationship devoid of trust, care or comfort. A shared phone also evokes the same thoughts within me. A phone is for contacting people, including your spouse; how can you do that if you share the same phone? Unless, of course, you're together all of the time, which is what a controlling partner wants.

● They may move you far away from your family so that it's harder to visit them. Taking you physically away from support makes sure you're in a more subdued, submissive state when they do ramp up their abuse. In my relationship, when the abuse got especially horrific, my partner would goad me with 'Go run to your mother,' knowing full well I couldn't. Lots of people who have opened up to me about their own experiences have told me how relocating was one of the first things their partner suggested at the beginning of the relationship. Some of them agreed and moved, others didn't, but the intent was still there - the abuser sought to move their victim further away from any support they had.

● Making up lies about you to others. It was only after my relationship ended with my abuser that I found out the true extent of how much he held a smear campaign against me. He told people I was crazy, he even told people I was violent, and to stay away from me. I was shocked when I heard this, and I felt so incredibly hurt and angry that for such a long time, horrible lies were being spread about me. My ex would also tell other women I was a cheater (which was him deflecting his own actions onto me), in order to gain sympathy from them. I don't know why this revelation came as such a shock to me, seeing as this is the exact thing he told me about his ex before me.

● Monitoring your phone calls with your family, going as far as cutting the line off if they feel like people are getting concerned about you or want to intervene. The amount of phones and laptops my ex smashed up because of me speaking with family and friends is too many to count on both hands. From throwing my phone into a bath full of water, to throwing it onto the roof or out of the bedroom window, his controlling acts certainly got more creative each time; one time he even took all the keys off of the keyboard laptop. These psychotic acts were all in the name of isolation.

● Convincing you that your family doesn't want you. In some extreme cases, the abuser can make you turn against your own family. My abuser latched onto things I'd told him about my childhood, and used these things to convince me that my family didn't really love me and that I was a burden to them. He used my own experiences and insecurities against me in order to gain full control over me.

Flag #2. Monitoring your activity.

Abusers will pursue coercive control through attempts to make themselves present everywhere. Even if you know deep down that your abuser isn't around, you may still have that feeling that you're being watched and monitored. Even when I went to the shop to pick up some things, I'd avoid speaking to anyone I knew for fear of my ex finding out. If I went home and saw his face like thunder, I knew I'd done something 'wrong' - had I been too friendly with the cashier? Did I spend too long at the shop? Had someone tried to call me while I was out, and he was mad because of this? These thoughts would race through my mind as a sick feeling filled the pit of my stomach, knowing what was going to come next.

Abusers will make themselves wherever you are by being unashamedly invasive.

They've been known to wire the victim's house with cameras or recording gadgets, some going as far as using two-way surveillance so they can speak to their victim at home throughout the day. Boundaries tend to not exist for a controlling spouse - invasive surveillance is usually placed in private areas such as the bathroom and bedroom. Not only is this a violation of freedom, it's downright degrading for the victim. This adds an extra element of control for the abuser, who wants to remind their partner: *they're watching*.

Flag #3. Denying your freedom.

A spouse exerting coercive control will often try to control your independence.

Some of their methods include:

- Trying to prevent you from going to work or school. This was the case for me, and it's a recurring theme that pops up when I talk to others who've been involved with a controlling partner. From going into moods when I went to work, to flying into rages about the people at work who I was 'having an affair with' or smashing up the house before I was due to go for an interview - my ex felt it acceptable to throw these frightening tantrums to stop me leaving. More often than not, his rages did stop me from leaving. The rare occasion that it didn't, he made my life a living hell. That was my punishment for daring to disobey his control over me.

- Restricting or taking away your access to transportation. I spoke to someone recently who told me her partner took her car to the garage to get it fixed, but returned empty handed. He told her it was beyond repair, seeing as it would cost too much to fix, and with the car being old it was dangerous. He said he'd take care of it all, and that he would drive her to wherever she needed to go. Of course, that offer fell through pretty quickly. She can no longer easily drive to town or meet up with her friend for a coffee, as he is always too busy to take her anywhere. When it's clearly not an inconvenience to him, her partner will fly into a rage if she asks to be taken somewhere and frighten her into submission. She even went as far as to apologize for asking, which he accepted!

● Stalking you when you're out. I've certainly experienced this one, and if you have too, you'll know just how unsettling and frightening it is. From looking over your shoulder to making sure you don't take a route home that'll upset your controlling spouse, the unease you feel when you think you're being followed is immense. It can make you behave in strange ways, hoping each move you make won't anger or provoke your abuser. What makes it all the more difficult to deal with is the fact that the source of this unease is your partner - the same person you're returning home to, the same person who'll you'll cook dinner for or who'll be waiting for you at home. When I was in the midst of my abusive relationship, my partner would stalk me when I was out, but he would deny it if I confronted him. He would know exactly where I'd been, how long I'd taken in each place and what route home I'd taken. But when I would ask if he was there or he saw me, he'd act defensive and insist he was at home at the time. This only fuelled my self-doubt, too, making me think I was going crazily paranoid. When I fled this relationship, he didn't care to hide his stalking; this became his way to try and keep control over me from afar.

● Taking your phone or insisting they know all your passwords. This is unbelievably common in controlling relationships. My partner knows my phone password, but that's not because he demanded it or set it himself - it's because I trust him, and if he needs to use my phone, he can. Rarely has he needed to, and I know when I leave the room, he's not flicking through my messages. However, this is a stark difference to how my ex behaved; not only did he set the password on all of my phones, tablets or laptops (when he wasn't smashing them), he would make sure I didn't know the password to his phone. Any time he thought I may have seen him enter it, he would change it. Of course, when I confronted him about this, he denied it. He would tell me he only knows my passwords because he set my phone up for me, and if I trusted him, I wouldn't need to know his password. One time, he even gave me an ultimatum: I could have the password to his phone, if I really wanted it. I could look through his phone. But, that meant I didn't trust him, so the relationship was over if I chose to do that. This type of manipulation moves me onto the next flag quite aptly:

Flag #4. Gaslighting.

The abuser must always be right, and they will make sure they force their victim to acknowledge this as fact. They'll go to great lengths to manipulate, lie, and g[1]aslight to convince you that you're wrong and to make sure they get their own way.

As an example of this, my ex once asked me to make steak for dinner before he left for work. When he came home that evening, I'd cooked the steak (like he'd asked) but he looked at it like it was completely foriegn - he screwed his face up as I went to serve him the steak he'd specifically asked for. He seemed annoyed, and told

---

1. https://www.healthline.com/health/gaslighting

e he'd asked for pasta for dinner, but he would 'make do' with the eak, despite not wanting it. When we sat at the table, he threw his nife and fork down after taking a bite of his food, and began to emand why I couldn't follow simple instructions.

recall he said he wanted steak, because it needed to be cooked at evening or we'd have to throw it out. I specifically recall him ying that as he unlocked the door before heading out that morning. ut, regardless of me knowing this to be the truth, he managed to onvince me he didn't say that - he said *pasta*. After a barrage of buse aimed at my intellect, I apologized and made him the pasta he riginally requested (despite the fact that he didn't).

his manipulation makes you question your own memory of events, nd the more frequently this happens, the more you find that you're asting doubt over your own ability to accurately remember onversations. This makes it much easier for the abuser to nanipulate you and make you think you're going crazy, which suits heir needs perfectly.

lag #5. Putting you down and calling you names.

Nasty put-downs, vile name-calling, and constant criticisms are all ypes of bullying behavior that a controlling spouse will often utilize o beat you down emotionally. They're designed with a cruel purpose o make you feel unimportant and lacking in anything of worth. It's lifficult to know this whilst you're enduring it. During the horrific erbal abuse, you're more inclined to believe it and know it as your ruth. If you get called 'dumb', 'stupid', 'worthless', 'a burden', 'fat', ugly' - whatever your abusers' chosen words of cruelty are - then eventually you begin to accept this as your reality.

The more you're beaten down and berated, the easier it is for you abusive partner to control you. They don't need to work so hard on their manipulation or lies when you're already a shell of a human being. You'll be less inclined to put up any resistance to the controlling behavior or vile treatment of you if you're already shadow of the person you were. All it takes is the same cutting insul to be thrown at you repeatedly.

Flag #6. Preventing or limiting your access to money.

I'll discuss this more in-depth later, but, simply put, controlling your finances is the abusers' way of moderating your freedom and you ability to leave the relationship. Some ways they'll utilize to obtai financial control include:

- Putting you on a tight (and very strict) budget that barely covers the essentials, such as food or clothing. Even if you are the breadwinner or have your own income, this won't stop an abuser from taking control of your money and deciding how much of it you can keep. In some cases, the abuser will leave their victim with little to no money of their own, whilst they spend it on things for themselves.

- Limiting your access to bank accounts, including your own. This can include stopping you from knowing your online banking passcodes, knowing your PIN numbers or even being able to open post from the bank. The less you know about money, the less inclined you'll be to try and use it to make a break for it.

● Hiding financial resources such as credit cards or paperwork is another tactic a controlling spouse will use to keep their victim in their grasp.

● Obsessively monitoring what you spend is a common theme in abusive relationships. The abuser will need to know how much you've spent, where, and why. If your answers don't meet their expectations or approval, then a bout of rage often ensues.

Flag #7. Turning your kids against you.

If you have children with the abuser (or even if you had children with someone else) they may try to use them as weapons against you. They may tell them you're a bad parent, make you out to be cruel or difficult, or they might belittle you in front of them.

This can create a rift in the relationship between you and your children, and will absolutely make you feel powerless with nowhere to turn. This can especially be the case when they successfully turn your children against you, encouraging them to be cruel or disrespectful towards you. The hurt this causes is like a dagger to the heart - not only is your spouse abusing you, they're actively encouraging (or allowing) you children to be mean and insulting towards you. The worthless feeling this instills only strengthens the abusers control over you.

Flag #8. Controlling aspects of your health, body, or routine.

A controlling spouse can monitor and control what and how much you eat, the time you're allowed to sleep, or how long you spend in the bathroom. Your abuser may go as far as requiring you to count calories whilst preparing your meals or they may ensure you adhere to a strict exercise routine. It's not uncommon for an abusive controlling partner to also control what medications you're allowed to take and whether you can go for medical care if you need it. These things all go towards stripping you of ownership of your own body and eventually, you feel as if your body is no longer yours.

You may feel as though you're always walking on eggshells and that your body is no longer your own.

Flag #9. Jealous accusations.

With clear jealousy and a need for control, the abuser will complain about the amount of time you spend with family or friends, either on or offline, is a manipulative way for them to phase out and lessen your contact with 'outsiders'. Eventually this phasing out leads to completely shunning those who you're closest to.

Mentioning that you want to see these people, or miss them, or would like to go to a social event can lead to your abuser making you feel guilty for suggesting such a thing. To escalate this further it's common for a controlling partner to make (often absurd accusations about you and another person - in my experience it was a work colleague, a cashier from the local coffee shop, another coworker after that... there were a number of people my ex accused me of having an affair with. He'd offer up astonishing reasons why he came to the conclusion I was having an affair, but he had me controlled and manipulated in such a way that I'd still end up apologizing - despite never having an affair of any kind. He'd make me think that my actions caused his paranoia, and this made me hundred times more careful of what I said or did, for fear of being accused of some untruth.

Flag #10. Threatening children or pets.

If their threatening demeanor stops working as effectively as they'd like towards you, the abuser may try to use threats against things you care about in an attempt to control you. For example, your children or pets may be at risk from their malicious, malignant behavior.

This can come in the form of making direct violent threats against the things you care for. It could be that they threaten to call social services to tell them you're a bad parent who neglects their children, or that you beat them. Despite you knowing this to be an outright lie, it still makes you fearful as your controlling partner can be so manipulative. It could be that your abuser threatens to take your children away from you, or kidnap them, and they may say the same about any pets you have.

Regardless of their cruel threat, the intent is the same: to make you submit to them through fear.

Chapter Three The Devastating Impact the Effects of Coercive Control Has on You and How to Deal with Them

—————

—————————

The only people who get upset by you having boundaries are the same people who benefit by you not having any."

THERE'S NO DENYING the devastation that coercive control h
on you. It slowly but very surely makes its way into your being, takir
over your mind, your body and eventually your spirit. Happine
seems so far away; feeling just okay or secure in your relationsh
would be a welcome change. The hollow being that this abuse mol
you into is a far cry from the person you were when you met yo
toxic partner. Even the most outgoing, confident, and self-assure
people aren't immune from the clutches of a controlling, abusi
spouse.

I'm going to outline the life altering effects that a controlli
relationship has on the victim so I can offer a little guidance on ho
to deal with these (or at the very least, how to best rationalize it
your head.) As you may know, a controlling spouse will manipula
you so much that your mind feels like a misty space where nothi
makes much sense at all - least of all what you're thinking. Maki
choices without fear, being able to put things in perspective, ar
being sure of your own thinking become a rarity when you'
endured the controlling abuse of a toxic partner, so let me try to blo
away some of that fog. I've segregated the effects of coercive contr
into two sections: the first is the day-today effects you endure
living with a controlling spouse; I'll call these 'lifestyle effects'. T
second is the effects it has on you as a human being, and how t
abuse makes you think and feel. I'll label these 'personal effects'.

Part 1: The Lifestyle Effects

Lifestyle Effect #1: Your social network starts to fritter away as you're discouraged from communicating with friends and relatives.

IN A CONTROLLING RELATIONSHIP, anything that threatens to take away the power the abuser has over their victim is to be eliminated. Resources, people that can help and family members are the first to be ticked off the abuser's hit list of things to be eradicated.

Lifestyle Effect #2: You are responsible for the relationship's health. You will be blamed if things don't go the abuser's way.

The troubles, concerns, and insecurities you have in the relationship? The ones that were born out of the abusive behavior you endure? These are for you to be burdened with because they are *your* fault. The state of the relationship is in your hands, according to the abuser, and if it's unhealthy, that's because of you.

Lifestyle Effect #3: You're doing things you don't want to do, out of fear of upsetting your partner

Doing things you don't want to do, or things way out of your comfort zone, just to appease your spouse is a big effect (not to mention a warning sign) of a controlling relationship. When you find that you're behaving in ways that you know aren't *you,* or doing things that you find uncomfortable, to prove yourself to your partner, this tends to have somewhat of a snowball effect. The abuser will push to break down more boundaries, and the things you find yourself doing to please your controlling other half are now done out of fear. Eventually, you aren't just doing things you don't want to do to please your abuser, but you're doing them out of fear of the repercussions if you don't. This doesn't necessarily mean violence either; verbal lashings and emotional manipulation hold just as much weight as physical aggression in controlling couplings.

Lifestyle Effect#4: You're not doing things you used to like doing, for fear of upsetting your partner

This can start with seemingly small things, like not going to the gym because your partner wants to 'spend more time with you' or you not partaking in your hobbies anymore as your abuser doesn't deem them appropriate. This escalates as the relationship develops with you being forbidden to do more things that appear to upset disrespect, or offend your partner. The 'small things' you're prevented from doing can begin to evolve into day-today restrictions on your life - *don't visit this area, make sure you're only 15 minutes, don't speak to such-and-such, don't drink any coffee it's bad for you, don't eat that food because it's fattening.*

Lifestyle Effect #5: You are being 'micromanaged' - your partner wants to know where you are at all times

UPDATES VIA PHONE CALL or text are expected if you need to do something that doesn't involve your partner. In my case, a text had to be followed up with a phone call, so my ex could hear my surroundings. If I said I was at the supermarket, I would have to call him up and he would assess if the background noise sounded like a supermarket. If another man's voice was heard in the background then God help me when I got back home. I learned to go stand by a till when I called him so he could hear the beeping of the checkout

Even just typing that brings back a flood of old memories of the insane things I would have to do to try and keep my abuser pacified.

Lifestyle Effect #6: You live under the threat of, or may suffer from physical or sexual violence

This one is more common than the internet or statistics will show you. Whilst we can often find comfort in knowing we aren't alone, the stats on this one, I don't believe, are anywhere near the accurate represtntion of the number of women who are suffering from physical or sexual violence in controlling relationships. I know from having conversations and discussions with those who've reached out to me via social media that a lot of unreported violence that goes on. On top of this, many victims can't and won't admit to the extent of the violence they endured, even after acknowledging that abuse *had* taken place. The threat of this kind of abuse is like an invisible set of strings that are tied to you and held above you by your abuser, controlling your actions to ensure you are complying with their expectations and demands of you.

Lifestyle effect #7: You live with incessant criticism which erodes your confidence in yourself and your abilities

NOTHING YOU DO IS RIGHT, you can't seem to make your abuser happy, and anything you do seems to be met with a barrage of insults, covert put-downs or, at best, absolute indifference. The critique of you isn't always outright nastiness, either (although a lot of the time it can be); your abuser may mock your weight whilst telling you it's because they care about your health. They may joke about what you're wearing, but only because they don't want you to embarrass yourself' by wearing such an outfit. They may offer compliments with undertones of criticism, such as, 'this meal isn't too bad, *for your standards*'. The nasty put-downs don't always have to be so thinly veiled, either, and can often be seen in the form of outright nasty, hurtful comments that are designed to really knock your confidence for six in one shattering blow. A controlling partner often isn't afraid to get personal, either - they'll use things against you that they know will really hit a nerve, such as family or events that have affected you in the past.

Part 2: The Personal Effects

Personal Effect #1: Social isolation

BEING CHASTISED FOR retaining contact with friends and family is an all-too-painful reality for many victims of a controlling partner. Keeping you at arms length from those that care about you is to ensure the abuser has the maximum amount of control over you as possible. Having no one to turn to, talk to, or help you is a huge benefit for the controlling spouse. The less support their victim has, the less likely they'll consider trying to break free. It rarely stops at friends and family, either; you are restricted in who you can speak to, are punished for becoming 'too friendly' with those outside of the relationship and find that it's easier if you just didn't bother with anyone except your abuser; that way, your life is easier, even if it's not *really* your life anymore.

Personal Effect #2: Loss of self-esteem and self-confidence

ven the most self-assured, confident, aspiring people aren't immune the devastating effects of a controlling, abusive spouse. The esence of esteem and confidence must be eradicated from the ctim in order for the abuser to take on full and total control, owing them to feel sheer dominance. From second (and third d fourth) guessing your decisions, to feeling like you're not good ough, to feeling unable to do anything right, your entire being is w filled and fuelled by insecurity and uncertainty in your own ilities.

Personal Effect #3: Physical and psychological damage

NG AFTER I FLED MY abusive partner, I found I was still nding the psychological damage he had created, even after I ought I was over it. Sure, I was over *him*, but I found I was still ling from the emotional torture he put me through. I couldn't ten to certain songs or it would remind me of an episode of abuse, a hurtful accusation he fired my way, or it would remind me something that once devastated me. When I got into a new ationship, I was naturally guarded, but some of the things my ex ummed into me were still prevalent; I was asking if I could do nething so basic, like ask if I could get a drink. I'd ask if I could the bathroom. I'd offer my new partner timescales if I needed to out, promising to be back before a certain time, which I was so d to doing, for fear of upsetting my ex. It took a long time for me bathe with the door shut, as this was a huge deal to my ex; I was ver allowed privacy. These simple things (that were my right to do) re stripped from me, and it took a while to repair the damage and vire my brain.

Personal Effect #4: Loss of status as an independent and capabl[e] adult

From a once independent and successful young woman, my abusi[ve] ex turned me into the total opposite. My independence w[as] something I took pride in; I was self-sufficient, somewhat fearle[ss] and ready for the amazing life I had planned ahead of me. When [I] first met my abusive ex, I thought he was another exciting part [of] my journey in life, and he seemed to be perfect for me. He cam[e] across as kind, funny, thoughtful, and understanding. As the mont[hs] passed, this train of thought was slowly getting turned on its hea[d]. My future plans were getting squashed for fear of losing my partn[er]. My career was put on hold to appease my abuser. My social circle w[as] slowly diminishing. My ability to do anything remotely independe[nt] or positive was removed from the short list of things I could [do] that wouldn't upset my controlling partner. I stood in my abuse[r's] merciless shadow, not daring to step out in case I awoke t[he] frightening side of him that I was so keen to keep at bay.

My story is similar to lots of men and women in a controlli[ng] relationship,, and whilst we all have our own version of events a[nd] experiences, the way we were made to feel is eerily similar in ea[ch] of our cases. It's like we become incapable of being our own pers[on] slowly but surely morphing into a subservient, internally-coweri[ng] victim of an all-consuming abuser.

Chapter Four Financial Coercion: Understanding Financial Abuse in a Controlling Relationship

"Financial abuse is a form of domestic violence"

FINANCIAL ABUSE IS so rarely talked about yet is so prevalent in controlling relationships. In cases where the abusive partner exerts excessive financial control or exploitation, it's undeniably difficult for the victim to speak up about it - with there being so little information out there about it, and even less people talking about it, it's a hard thing to seek advice on.

Too often I've spoken to victims where their financial institutions failed to acknowledge the financial abuse that was so clearly going on; for example their mortgage provider. In a contractual arrangement between a business and a couple, I understand that it's not easy for the company to act upon information that delves into the privacy of a tricky relationship situation. For a while, I worked at a bank, and we had one customer who was so clearly being abused by her spouse, and we were limited as to what we could do to help as we 'couldn't be seen to take a side'. The abuser in this case would spend their money for the mortgage, resulting in us calling the victim every month to chase the payment. This would result in her spouse getting mad at her, so we agreed with her to only call her between set hours when he wasn't there. She acknowledged herself the damaging effect of his abusive, controlling behavior was having, not only on her emotionally, but financially too - still, there was little we could do to help. Our hands were tied, despite it being so plain to see how much she just needed someone to reach out and give her a helping hand. I wanted so badly to speak to this woman human-to-human, but this isn't something that was allowed, as the company needed to remain impartial. Similarly, it's not easy for victims to approach these companies and seek help or a resolution to their situation.

On top of this, financial abuse is rarely reported on in the media, and from what I've seen, it's not very well researched by advice givers either. Whilst other forms of abuse have (quite rightly) been scrutinized and exposed, financial abuse has remained somewhat buried. I feel like it's because it's perhaps seen as being 'less extreme' or 'less damaging' than domestic violence. Perhaps it's because it's less obvious in situations involving joint accounts and household bills - nobody can see from the outside looking in. It may be less understood because there is no real definition, no official 'criteria'.

Regardless, it's not uncommon. And it's certainly not just another 'unfortunate' by-product of an unhealthy relationship - it's real and it's hugely important for it to be recognized.

Financial abuse can take many forms, and like coercive control as a whole, it's certainly not black and white or one-size-fits-all. I've managed to group them into three classifications of sorts; direct financial harm, severe financial control, and the exploitation of joint financial resources. Upon research and talking to women who've endured this, I've found the most common forms of specific financial abuse involve the abuser taking credit in the victim's name, followed by non-payment or lack of contribution to joint bills, as well a draining accounts and other assets. A lot of the time, the victim will be experiencing multiple forms of financial abuse at once.

During my time working at the bank, I found there was a lack of understanding (or at least a willingness) to consider financial abuse and it seems this theme continues throughout most other financial companies. Frustratingly, this can leave the victim in a dire financial situation, responsible for debts they never agreed to, completely at the mercy of their abuser who controls and accesses the money as they please, and ultimately prolonging their suffering at the hands of a controlling partner.

Financial abuse is undeniably complex and it does vary from situation to situation, but as I mentioned, I did manage to somewhat 'categorize' it in order to make it easier to digest. I did this from lengthy conversations with victims of this type of abuse, a lot of reading up on the subject, as well as my own experiences with my finances being controlled and withheld.

These are the most common scenarios of financial abuse that cropped up in my conversations:

The abuser not contributing to joint bills, even if they could do so easily.

The abuser forcing or persuading the victim to take out credit.

The abuser using up all of the joint resources available.

The abuser ensures they have access to the victim's income, banking and any savings, and controlling these.

The abuser controlling and/or interfering with the victims benefits.

Let me discuss more about the 'categories' of abuse.

1. Abuse that causes the victim direct financial harm

This sees the victim is left with less (if any) money, assets or even property within their control. An obvious (and extremely cruel) example is where the abuser directly steals money from the victim. This could of course range from a small amount of money, leading to a systematic, ongoing pattern of financial abuse amounting to large sums. This was the case for me, whereby my money would be taken from me, if I liked it or not. I can't say it was all of the time, but it was regular. My partner knew my PIN for all of my cards, and would use my money for drinking binges. He would create an argument in order to storm out of the house, taking my card with him. Invariably, his spending of my money (which left me with nothing) would be my fault; I drove him to it.

It's not just when you're in the clutches of an abusive relationship, either; abusers will, and can, control from afar, and I spoke to one man who had been with his partner for almost four decades who told me his story. He was in his late fifties, and for most of the time in his relationship, had been the victim of physical and emotional abuse from his (now former) partner. She had always controlled the finances, and after she'd paid the bills and taken 'her cut' of the money, he was left with a very small amount of his wage each month. This meant he was unable to save or put anything aside each month for emergencies. When he eventually left his ex, she would still continue her abuse of his finances from afar. He ended up

ith no money in his bank account as his ex-partner had completely
nptied it, leaving him with no option but to go to a food bank.
he had stolen his passport and his computer during the split, too,
though she denied this by insisting he had taken them. Horribly,
is woman was intent on being cruel and controlling despite no
nger being in a relationship with her victim. It's an all too common
eme that abusers try to hold onto the reins of control even after the
lationship has ended.

lso spoke to a woman in her thirties who had, after many years,
ally found the courage to seek access to legal aid. She was trying
escape her controlling abuser, who was not only domineering
notionally, but also physically. Late last year her husband moved
t with two of her children, leaving one behind - to create as much
artache and chaos as he could, she told me. However, for the
e of her children and her own sanity, she took her husband back
The abuse continued, most recently with the husband taking
r credit cards and even seeking out power of attorney over her
ances. She had been to see a solicitor to see what help she was
gible for, but heartbreakingly, she was told that her situation was
emed to be not "extreme enough" to qualify for any kind of legal
I.

causing direct financial harm, the thing I've encountered most
quently is for the abuser to force the victim to take out credit.
similar method used in this type of abuse is for the abuser to
nsfer liabilities into their victim's name. This then frees them of
y liability but essentially forces their victim into even more debt.

ese methods of abuse veer slightly away from direct theft, hiding
destruction of cards or paperwork. Instead the abuse burdens debt

or liability on the victim, who is then left to pay the loan or debt o
thus causing direct financial harm, even sometimes long after leavin
the relationship.

I spoke to another woman who told me about the issues she w
left with after her ex took out three payday loans. She explained th
she had never applied for these loans and that the applications we
made fraudulently using her phone by her ex-partner. She only four
out about these loans after she and her ex had split up. Both tl
payday lenders that she had this debt with were chasing her for tl
unpaid money, despite her informing them of the fraud.

2. Financial abuse through severe financial control

The second type of abuse is caused through severe financial contro
As with all abuse, there's a wide range of the levels of abuse in the
cases, from the abuser using sporadic interference through to the
taking full-on, direct control, leaving the victim with absolutely i
financial freedom.

Of course, we all know it's common in relationships to have joi
bank accounts (for some, it's the norm). Therefore partners a
expected to have a good amount of co-control over joint resourc
For the most part, this works out fine; couples in healthy, trusti
relationships find that this is the best way to deal with financ
However, for the calculating abuser in a controlling relationship, tl
is merely yet another way to maintain power and dominance ov
their victim.

A woman messaged me last year about her partner, who she'd le
who was still visiting her address to demand money. If she did
pay him, he would turn violent on her and trash the property. S

felt like she couldn't seek help from the police as they'd been useless before. So she was giving him money every month, just to save herself from a beating.

Another shocking story was from a lady who'd told me her entire journey with her controlling spouse. Thankfully, she'd left him years prior, but gave me an insight into the situation she had been in whilst they were together. He was never physically abusive, she told me, but the underlying threat of violence was always there, and he was inclined to smash objects when he was upset. The part of her story that really shocked me was when her ex partner persuaded her to ask for money from her relatives in order to pay for their 'wedding'. This wedding never happened, despite him promising her it would; he then went on to use the money to pay his debts.

Another form of severe financial control is the abuser demanding that the victim account for all of their spending.

A woman who reached out to me told me how her husband persuaded her to take out a loan against the family home and start a business with him, putting all the financial transactions in her name alone. The business was eventually made bankrupt. After she was discharged from bankruptcy, her partner was still insisting that all the money, including any benefits, needed to go into his account. He controlled her expenditure, not permitting her to spend (her money) or buy things for her children.

Also in this category are incidences of the abuser interfering with the victim's employment, which was also the case for myself. It's a frustrating irony when your abuser takes your money but also forbids you from working due to their own paranoia and insecurity. I hear of a lot of this type of abuse, most recently from a woman who had to make herself and her children homeless in order to get help; her husband stopped her from working, which meant she was trapped financially in her relationship. She felt her only way out was, to quote her, 'go further than rock bottom'. The police stepped in, and after she told them her situation, she found help wasn't as far away as she thought. She hasn't seen her abuser since, thankfully.

3. Exploitation of joint resources

The last type I'm going to discuss is where the abuser exploits the joint financial resources that are available in a relationship. In a world where it is entirely normal to have joint household bills and joint accounts and liabilities, there is a line where the joint resources are exploited by the abuser. Where that line is could end up being subject to debate, but I'll aim to offer a flavour of this type of financial abuse in this segment.

In a relationship where there are bills to be paid towards the household there is somewhat of a grey area in terms of how finances are arranged and bills are split. However, it is also common from my own experience, and from other survivors I've spoken to, for non-contribution towards the payment of bills to become an ongoing form of abuse even once the relationship has completely broken down. I still had arrears to pay off for months after I left my abusive ex, serving as a nasty reminder of the controlling relationship I had endured.

Last year, a single mother messaged me for advice and I asked her a little more about her situation. She advised me she was separated from her husband who had been abusive to her and emotionally abusive to their daughter, which resulted in her leaving him after almost ten years. Her husband had managed all of the finances, and she believed he was paying the bills - but he wasn't. Sadly, all of the bills were in her name, as her husband had bad credit. She was now liable for all the debts, including rent arrears, despite her not living in that property anymore. Fortunately, her situation has improved, but she still had to pay off all of the debt he accumulated in her name.

I read another similar story in the news earlier this year, too. Whilst the main story wasn't about financial abuse, it did contain a strong example of commonplace financial abuse. Her relationship had broken down due to domestic violence and she moved out of the property she shared with her abuser. Her ex was still harassing her by text, phone, and social media, as well as turning up uninvited to her mother's home where she was staying. Her ex was still living in their shared rental property, but he had stopped paying the rent altogether. She was then liable for the arrears due on the property, despite her not living in it. The story I read was more about the physical side of the abuse she endured, but the emotional torment, stress, and worry of financial abuse was laced throughout the article; it just wasn't labelled as such.

Another example of the exploitation of joint resources is from when I worked at the bank. A young woman sought advice from us, bravely calling in to let us know of her situation and how we could help. She had separated from her violent partner earlier that year. She had a restraining order against him, which prevented him from contacting her. However he was still able to draw money out of their joint bank account, repeatedly making it overdrawn and taking her money out as soon as it arrived in her account. She contacted us to ask us to freeze the account, however at the time, we could not do this without her partner being there as well - which was impossible since not only did she have a restraining order on him, he wouldn't comply with freezing the account. Bear in mind, this was many years ago and I know banking regulations have changed in order to acknowledge and support those enduring financial abuse, but this kind of controlling behavior from afar is still going on. Plenty of victims, unlike the one who called in to us, wouldn't have the courage to call their bank and let them know of the abuse they were enduring; they'd prefer to suffer in silence than open up about such personal things that they're possibly ashamed of.

———

THE PURPOSE OF THIS chapter is to bring light to something I feel is rarely discussed when talking about abusive relationships, yet it's so common. For some reason, articles and blogs on the topic of abuse and coercive control don't delve into this topic; possibly because it can be quite complex and has a lot of grey areas.

Chapter Five Breaking the Spell of Control

═══

"Confusing control with love leads you to unhappiness"

You picked this book up for a reason; were you just trying to figure out if your partner was controlling, or looking for some validation for your gut instinct? Perhaps you know you're in a controlling partnership and wanted some comforting words from someone who has been there. Or, you may have been looking for ways you can break free from the cloud of control hanging over you. Whatever your reason for choosing this book, this chapter can help you. You already know, at the very least, there's something unhealthy about your relationship, or you wouldn't be reading this book. On the other end of the spectrum, you may be readying to leave your abuser. This chapter serves to help you in your plight to break free of the controller, and offer you the tools to place yourself at the helm of your vessel, with you controlling your own actions.

It goes without saying, really, that your plan of action will vary depending on your level of entanglement with your abuser. Leaving a relationship that's decades upon decades old is different than leaving a relationship that's weeks old. But once you have recognized a controlling partner, and you know you need to make changes, then please read on for my guidance.

First of all, you need to **assess your level of safety.**

For most people, leaving a relationship can often just mean a fe
uncomfortable conversations about the demise of the relationshi
followed by an otherwise clean break. For many of us in abusi
relationships, though, the controlling behavior will last during tl
breakup and persist afterwards, often becoming threatening.

A controlling partner will be outraged at your audacity to lea
them, meaning they may try to up their controlling behavior, whic
can show itself in the form of not only aggression and threats, b
also grief - although, they're not grieving for the person they lo
- they're grieving for the control they've lost. A controlling spou
tends to have plenty of tricks up their sleeve.

To break it down, the abuser is threatened by their ultimate fear:
lack of control, and being left by someone opens them up to th
fear becoming a reality. It's important to be honest with yourself, ar
that means being realistic about what your partner could be capab
of. I've mentioned this a thousand times before in other books, b
please, please, no matter what - document your concerns, at the ve
least. Ideally diarize the abuse. Even if you have no intention
ever involving the law, be sure to document what you're enduring
remember the law is there to protect you. Even if you're not at a poi
where you're ready to leave, or even if you can't imagine this ev
being a possibility, it is important to think about a safety plan. If y
are in the clutches of a controlling relationship, the risk of escalati
is always looming.

Assemble a support system in whichever way you can. It doesn't ne
to be sophisticated or as difficult as it sounds. Despite being, by yo
partner's design, blocked from contacting friends and isolated fro
family, this can be done. If you've not been stopped entirely fro

seeing loved ones, you may find that your partner disapproves of this, and aren't afraid to let you know. This, too, may encourage you to create a barrier between yourself and those who care about you.

On top of this your embarrassment or discomfort with the worrying aspects of your relationship may have made you feel like you had to paint a happier picture to friends and family than was the reality. Perhaps you felt too intimidated or too ashamed to tell them what's really been happening behind closed doors. Or, perhaps, it's the fear of being disbelieved? Not being taken seriously is a big fear that I can totally relate to, particularly if you've been giving others the impression that your partnership is happy; *perfect,* even. I can't take these feelings away from you, and there is only one thing that can: Taking a deep breath and speaking up. You want to make changes, at the very least - it's why you're reading this book. It is so important that if you want to make real, positive changes in your situation, that you strengthen your ties to people you feel you can trust. If you feel like you've burned all of your bridges, you likely haven't - my confidante was a coworker. I took a leap of faith and divulged my situation to her, because I thought I had no-one else. By opening up to her, it not only gave me someone to back my version of events up (if needed), but it gave me a jolt of newfound confidence - I felt heard, like I'd purged some of the toxicity within me, and I also felt clarity for the first time in a long time.

As well as this, I'd recommend telling your doctor. Not only can they help, it's another person who can corroborate your story should they ever need to. They can refer you to places that can help you pick yourself up mentally, offer you help directly and it's all confidential. As judged and as nerve-wracking as it may be to open up to your doctor like this, I urge you to do it. Utilize the help that's there. Step out from the controlling shadow you're standing behind and take back your power. As hard as it feels, it does get easier - the hardest step, as with anything, is always the first one.

Take the time to think about your short-term and long-term plans. Pause for a few moments now even to think about your future. If you are going to leave the household, what are the financial considerations you need to tackle? Where can you stay, or what actions do you need to take in order to get a place of your own? Think about what possessions or belongings you'll need. If you are going to ask your partner to leave, what legal (and physical) protection will you have in place if they flat out refuse? These are difficult things to think about, and no one situation is the same as another, so your considerations will be different to another victim of a controlling abuser. It's freeing to take your head out of the sand and think about these things, and taking the time to do so helps motivate you to prepare for the possibility of escaping hasilty if needed.

A few people who have opened up to me about their abusive partner have told me they are going to give their controlling spouse an 'ultimatum'. Whilst, personally, I'm not a big fan of these, if you're considering going down this route, you should do so with a plan. If you are going to set an ultimatum, such as your partner seeking help, or you going to counselling together, you need to give them a timescale to meet this. Vocalize this and make it clear, and their reaction will tell you a lot about how the ultimatum is going to go. In the same breath, it's not uncommon for a manipulative controller to bait and switch in these circumstances. They'll agree to every boundary and ultimatum put in place, only to ramp up their abuse and punish you for ever considering taking your power back.

If there are children involved, you will need to consider how you will keep them physically and emotionally safe. It might be a good idea to know what you will tell them when the separation occurs so you're not made to feel like you have to lie or sugarcoat things to the point of confusion. These things I'm asking you to consider are not intended to make you fearful or you or paralyze you into not taking any action; it's the complete opposite, the more you think about the logistical challenges of the changes you're wanting to make happen, the less likely they are to stop you in your tracks. In short, be prepared and understand the predictability of your partner. These two things together equate to more power in your hands.

I know that making up your mind to go ahead and confront your spouse about controlling behavior or to leave the relationship is undeniably challenging. The right thing to do, as with a lot of life-changing decisions, can be far, far from the easiest. I can't think of a time in my life when it was more important for me to pay attention to my eating, sleeping, and mental health to keep up my strength. The mean paradox to this was that eating, sleeping, and my emotional health were at the bottom of a large list of anxieties and worries I had at that time. But I implore you: don't ignore your health. Even if it's just taking the dog for a walk, practice meditating, or taking a few minutes to listen to a song you enjoy (preferably from a time in your life where you were filled with hope or contentment). Or, in my case, it was also making sure that I stuck to my limits when drinking, and not finishing the bottle, only to open another one straight away. It's the seemingly small steps, on a daily basis, of taking care of yourself during this emotionally exhausting time that makes a big difference to your mental ability to take on the manipulation and game-playing of a controlling abuser.

At this point, I want to let you know that your emotions will likely be up and down like a rollercoaster. Not only that, your feelings can be mixed, jumping from one resolution to another, your thoughts contradicting one another. Rarely does someone swear to leave their toxic relationship or offer an ultimatum and retain their sense of resolve 100% of the time.

It's an all-too common story: You get inspired to leave a bad relationship, or even just motivated to sit down and have a real conversation with your spouse about their concerting behavior. Then, the next day, things can feel much scarier and you're filled with enough dread to put a halt to confronting your partner about their abuse. Or you've determined that your relationship is toxic and you need to leave as soon as you can, and then your partner senses that you're becoming detached, and they feel like you're pulling away from their clutches. This then provokes them to do something so apparently thoughtful or loving that you have second thoughts about your concerns. The better you can anticipate this, the higher the chances you are to go through with your original plan of action. That doesn't mean you need to bury your feelings, though: You don't need to be all-or-none about your relationship. That certainly won't help you, and being forgiving about your emotions and knowing they'll often be confusing is important. You can still acknowledge that there were good times in the relationship, otherwise you wouldn't have held onto the relationship as long as you have done. By taking the time to explore your fluctuation of emotions, this can help you understand how you fell into the abusive pattern, which is a cathric (albeit emotional) thing to do. By acknowledging this, you also offer yourself the tools to better avoid an abusive spouse in the future. Talk, write, think, even draw, about some of the things you will miss om the relationship, and have an understanding that you might not el so certain all day every day that you are doing the right thing. nat's part of the journey; You will be plagued with self-doubt, ncertainty, and anxiety that you're wrong. That's normal, because e abuse has conditioned you to feel this way. But, remember, you're king your power back, so wait out these doubtful times and your solve *will* return.

:aving an abusive relationship or even just trying to make changes one is a continuing process, not a one-off event. It takes your re, thought-out planning, and several steps. If your first attempt making changes or leaving has failed, don't despair and remain tangled in the abusive cycle. Take a breath, remember this isn't easy process, and give yourself a break. Know that failing in this esn't define you. Start again.

:member to keep your eye on your long-term goal; don't let the g take over your future plans. Whilst it's hard, try to keep a grasp your logic. Is this controlling person who you want to be with in ew months down the line, in a year, or 30 years? Are you willing give that much more of your care, energy, time, love, and life to meone who only seeks to dominate you? Each bit of progress you ake, no matter how small it may seem or feel, takes you closer to gaining your power and attaining the life that you truly deserve. It's t a failure to have your first attempt not work out as you planned it It's a chance to bolster your support, get everything in order, and rn from the challenges, then your next (or even ninth) attempt uld be the one that sticks. That attempt could be the one where ur life truly changes.

I can't lie to you and say once you're away from the abuse that it's a
over. It does take a long time to get over an abusive and controllir
relationship. Being mercilessly monitored, cruelly isolated, an
abused leaves its mark. But, recovery can and will take place.

You can start by reclaiming hobbies and interests that have bee
blocked or forbidden by your abuser. For instance, you may like t
go on walks alone, but were stopped from doing this whilst in
relationship. Imagine the liberation of being able to take a stroll c
your own whenever you pleased, and not having to answer to yor
controller when you return home.

When you're out of the relationship, you can begin a new journe
to seek out who you are as a person, without being manipulated c
gaslighted - you can embark on finding out who you truly are. Th
means being kind to your body and spirit. You can't move forwai
on this journey without taking care of yourself. In a controllir
relationship, you can become completely alienated from yor
physical self. For example, you may have no choice in what you es
when you eat, when you bathe, how long you can shower for,
you can do so in private, what you can wear... you may find th
you're so detached from your physical being that you can't imagii
experiencing feelings of vitality. Regardless, I recommend you {
walking, or take yoga classes, dance like you were forbidden fro
doing, do some light stretching, go for a jog in the woods... no matt
how little you feel like doing it.

Connect with others where you can, too. Don't say "no" or back aw
from social events if they're offered to you. Reconnect with fami
friends, and be sure to keep in touch with supportive professiona
As you're all too aware, abusers separate their victims from othe

deliberately. Reconnecting with old friends and taking the opportunity to make new ones sees you regain much-needed support and provides you with a sense of self again. I wasn't allowed contact with friends or family, If I got a text, my ex had to read it before me. If I spoke on the phone, I couldn't leave the room - I had to stay in the same room as him or he'd fly into a rage. Over time, I found it easier for me to shun and cut off those I was once so close to. This was to avoid my ex's control fuelled rages, but to also avoid letting my friends and family down any more; I'd always commit to seeing them but would never show up, as I knew this would upset my abuser. Eventually, as I became dependent on him for the majority social contact, my self esteem hit the floor. After their separation, I found that a lot of the people I'd cut contact with were happy to regain contact and even though it's a difficult conversation to reach out for, it's worth it.

This also gives you the opportunity to share the true story of the relationship, as much as you feel comfortable doing so. It can feel so empowering to express your truth and know you've been brave and strong enough to walk away from someone so toxic and cruel. If you can't open up to others, which is totally understandable, you can create a journal where you document your time in the relationship. Telling your true story - even if it's just to yourself - helps you cope with your feelings. Trust me - give it a go!

I'm a big advocate for expressing yourself creatively. It can be anything at all: Drawing. Singing. Painting. Gardening. Writing. Creating anything at all. It's too easy to shut down creatively during a controlling relationship, especially when you're attending to your partner's demands and being the person they insist you must be. Releasing your creative side is a great outlet, especially if you couldn't do it whilst in the relationship. can be a step on the path to recovery. I know a woman who, when she left her abuser, got her own apartment, and released her creativity in decorating her new place. She did everything herself; painting, tiling, even building her own office desk and shelves from scratch. She would never have been able to consider doing this whilst in her abusive relationship, as anything that looked like a hobby or outlet was forbidden. She wasn't allowed to work, and her days were spent cleaning the house and preparing food. From the outside, her life looked rosy; she had a big house, what seemed like an easy going life, and expensive holidays. However, she was trapped with her controlling spouse, fearful of how she would survive if she ever left. With little money, she got her own place, and had to get creative when it came to decorating it as she had little funding to do this. Out of this was born a new hobby, and one she has turned into a business. She upcycles furniture and sells it on social media now, making a living from what was her coping mechanism after leaving her abuser. Now that's her passion and her career, which is something she ought to be incredibly proud of.

Remembering the dark times can help us appreciate the present. You can compile a list of the controlling incidents that you've experienced, helping you understand what you've been through and appreciate your own strength. You can simply have moments (not too often, however) where you reflect. You can recall the horrific events, the mean things you endured, the manipulation you encountered, and the hurt and anxiety the relationship caused you. You aren't doing this torture yourself - it's a way to bask in the triumph of being able to overcome such a dark and toxic place.

You need to learn to put yourself at the top of your list of priorities now. After structuring your life around the abusers' demands and expectations, it can be incredibly difficult for you to remember your own opinions, beliefs, and wants. Abusers are able to convince their victims that their thoughts are stupid, not wanted, and wrong, leading victims to amend the way they view themselves and the world to fit their partner's wishes.

It's not uncommon to hear your abuser's critical voice in your head when being self-critical. It is so vital to begin to replace that voice with a compassionate, understanding, and kind one. After all, nobody but you can know the true cruelty handed to you by your abuser - show yourself some understanding and stop being so tough on yourself. Your abuser wants you to be filled with self-criticism, so do your best to shut this off whenever you find it creeping in.

It's completely natural for you to feel fear, guilt, and regret from time to time. Looking ahead will help eradicate these pointless emotions and offer you hope. Recovery does not happen overnight, just like the abuse and control didn't happen overnight. It's a process. But, I promise, the spell of abuse can be broken by you.

Chapter Six Coercive Control is Not Love: A Plea for You to Remember This

===

"Love is many, many things. But it's never toxic."

I want this chapter to just reaffirm how jealous and controlling behavior does not equate to love or care, no matter how much your abusive spouse says it does. Too many times, I've had people message me or start up conversations where they want some validation that their spouse is only acting so controlling because it's how they 'show love' or communicate their adoration. *'He only acts that way because he's scared of being without me deep down; he has abandonment issues,'* was how someone defended their partners actions more recently.

It can be all too easy to fall into that pit, too. Of course it's easier to believe that your partner just has emotions they can't express properly, or they have trauma that causes their abusive behavior. It's less harsh on your feelings that way - if you don't confront the grim reality, you don't have to deal with the inevitable outcome: leaving and never looking back. Or, sticking with an abuser who you'll have to accept will never change.

I wanted to break the chapters up with this stark but very important reminder, because not only is the abuser very good at manipulating our thoughts, they can also make it so we manipulate our own thoughts; doing their deceptive work so they can kick back and reap their rewards. After they fill our minds with their version of reality, it soon becomes a self fulfilling prophecy - we make that false reality happen for the abuser, which serves to keep up subdued.

Let me take this time to remind you what love is *not*.

Love is not **domination.** In loving, nurturing relationships, there is no 'master'. Dominance isn't a thing, because it's a true partnership. When you're in the midst of coercive control, there is a huge tipping of the scales in terms of power and domination, and the victim is always left as the obedient 'servant' in this scenario. When you're loved, properly, power doesn't even come into play. There's no dynamic that means you can be dominated, and decision making is a joint venture - your input is required, because it's valued and respected.

Love is not **manipulation.** This means not tugging on your heart strings to justify their vile, toxic and irrational behavior, making you feel like you deserve their treatment of you or making you believe falsehoods for their own gain. Of course, even healthy relationships have spats, misunderstandings, arguments, and sometimes people behave in ways they shouldn't. However, this should never be justified by way of manipulation - blaming their outburst of anger on sheer passion or stress. A controlling spouse and manipulation go hand in hand, and a manipulator is typically so good at their trade that it's hard to know when you're being manipulated or not. This shouldn't be an issue in a loving, trusting partnership, but it's sadly the day-to-day issues you face when living with a controlling spouse.

Love is not **physical abuse.** 'Look what you made me do, do you think I wanted to hit you?', or 'You really know how to rile me up' Have you heard that kind of talk after being physically assaulted by your spouse? What about, 'I just care so much that I can't control my actions, I don't mean it,' or 'I don't remember doing it, but it's when I feel like I'm losing you that I lash out'? No kind of physical abuse is excusable, nor should the burden of blame ever be placed on the victim. A lot of the time, this is the case, alongside the abuser insinuating their heightened emotions are because of the victim Physical abuse doesn't just mean hitting or punching, either grabbing, pushing, nipping, twisting your arm or face, biting... any unwanted physical contact in a threatening manner is abuse, because its purpose is just that: To abuse. To threaten. To instill fear and provoke the abusers desired behavior from you.

Love is not **intimidation.** I still remember the gut wrenching feeling of saying something in front of friends, and getting 'the look' off of my ex to tell me I 'd said the 'wrong thing'. He'd remain charming and friendly whilst we were with them, but the verbal abuse (at least) I'd get when we were on our own was enough to make me feel sick with fear. Thinking back to those times now, I never said anything 'wrong'; it was simple things that he deemed I was saying just to embarrass him, such as how much we paid for furniture or why we weren't having a holiday that year. I was so open and felt I had nothing to hide, but he was the complete opposite. I soon learned to keep my mouth shut or look to him for approval before I spoke. Intimidation can often be veiled behind jokes, too, and then when you get upset about it, the abuser can brush this off as you being 'too sensitive', 'boring', or someone who can't take a joke.

Love is not **mind games and game playing.** My ex would flaunt other potential partners in front of me, made me aware that he could leave when he wanted to, and left me walking on eggshells when I was uncertain as to what his next move would be. This anxiety-inducing feeling left me at his mercy, and he knew that. He'd take off for days on end, knowing I'd be panicking about what he was doing, but also knowing I'd be waiting for him when he returned. He would unfriend me on social media (petty yes, confusing, yes) just so I couldn't see what he was doing. Having to second guess if your partner is playing games is a horrible way to live through a relationship - in fact, it's not a relationship at all, it's a living nightmare.

Love is not, never has been and never will be, **control.**

On the flip side of this, let me tell you what love most certainly *is*.

Love is bound by **respect.** Your goals, ambitions, your boundaries... they're all acknowledged and respected. More than this, they're supported and nourished. You know you can have a difference of opinion with your spouse, and that's okay because you respect each other regardless. You can have your own hobbies and interests outside of the relationship and away from your partner because, not only is that healthy, but they respect it. They know you're passionate about other things, and because they love you, they encourage you to do what makes you happy.

Love is bound by **equality.** I don't necessarily mean you share bills 50/50; that's not always feasible in every relationship, as one partner will invariably earn more than the other. However, the breadwinner would never flout this. Equality is seen in the distribution of decision-making, housework, lifestyle choices, financial decisions, and family rules. You'd never be made to feel 'less than' or sub-par in a loving relationship.

Love is bound by **emotional integrity and honesty.** The complete opposite of mind games and manipulation. Not only should you be able to open up and be honest about how you're feeling to your partner, the same should be said for them. Unhappy, anxious, concerned, panicked, overthinking? You ought to be able to tell your spouse about these feelings, and know that the reception to this is one of openness and caring. Unlike a controlling relationship, where emotions are a currency used by the abuser, a loving relationship has a wealth of emotional integrity that sees honesty play a big part in mmunication. You can say how you feel, and you can be honest out insecurities and fears, knowing they are in safe hands.

ve is bound by **safety.** Like I mentioned before, we're human, so sagreements happen. Arguments can arise from misunderstanding frustrations outside of the relationship, but these can all be aired ithout the fear of abuse taking place. In a loving partnership, you low you can say how you feel and even if the response is a sagreeable one, you know this will be expressed in a non-violent, n-confrontational way. It all boils down to the respect element of ve; your partner respects what you have to say, and they also respect ur space and your safety. A truly loving relationship wouldn't tertain violence or the threat of it.

ve is bound by the **partnership** you build. Because that's what you ould be: Partners. In partnerships, 'no' means 'no'. Boundaries are spected. Being forced or manipulated to do things doesn't exist. u have an abundance of trust. Communication isn't held back or ed against you. Your interests are there to be explored. You are couraged, not exploited.

Chapter Seven Coercive Control After Separation

———

"The wound is the place where light enters you"

C ontrolling and abusive partners, as you know, don't let go of things easily, least of all what they need to dominate most of all: you.

This chapter isn't intended to frighten or upset, but to help you best prepare for the actions your abuser may take in the aftermath of the separation. The more you can prep for the malignant reaction you may face from your abuser, the better position you are in to shield yourself and your loved ones. Coercive control rarely ends the moment you leave, particularly if you have ties to your ex, such as children or even a business. I want this chapter to help you understand the post separation control an ex will try to hold over you; if you know what malicious tricks they're likely to use, you can be ready to tackle it head-on.

Harassment and Intimidation

Waiting for you outside of work, texting you threatening messages, sending messages to you via third parties, leaving ominous gifts at your doorstep, destroying your property, calling your relatives, spreading lies to your family about you... the list can go on and on. There, apparently, is no depth to which a controlling spouse won't sink to. They'll harass you and intimate you to let you know that they're still present, and they want to make you feel like they'll never go away. *They'll always be around, whether you like it or not*, is their message.

Stalking is a common behavior of jilted controlling exes, and is why I implore you to document every time you see your ex turning up or appearing unexpectedly. From ominously glaring at you from afar in a bar, to walking past your house repeatedly, to being in the same shop as you; if it doesn't feel right, write it down. As this compiles, it offers you a form of evidence to show the authorities, if needed. It also helps to show you that you aren't going mad; it'll serve to reassure you that you're most certainly being intimidated and you're not paranoid (which is a controlling spouse's line of choice when it comes to gaslighting you.)

Stalking is often associated with creepy men hiding in the shadows following their victim around whilst wearing a trench coat. This stereotypical view doesn't consider the reality of a stalking ex partner; a one that is emotionally obsessed and consumed with the need to control their victim. This kind of stalker doesn't try to hide. They don't lurk in the shadows (most of the time). They want to be seen. They want to sense your fear, make you retreat, and watch you squirm with sheer panic.

Where a restraining order has been granted, the abusive ex may resume the stalking, but from a 'safe' distance; the one that the law has demanded they don't encroach on. This way, they're not breaking the law, but are still able to get to you. If the restraining order makes it tougher for them to intimidate you via stalking, controlling partners are known to use third parties to do their dirty work. These are called 'flying monkeys', and these followers of the abuser are used to send threatening messages, insults, and abusive promises

These pawns can sometimes even be people you once trusted, which serves to make you feel powerless. However, throughout all of this, it's important to know you're not powerless - believe in your own resolve, it'll pull you through these terrible times.

Physical Violence

Even if your abusive relationship didn't include violence, or the violence was rare, the threat of it still remains when you're out of the relationship. The need to control is what fuels the abuser's behavior, and when you remove their ability to control you, their controlling behavior can be seen in bouts of aggression and violence. Where an abuser finds violence towards their victim doesn't offer the desired results, the manipulative controller will then threaten to carry out acts of violence on themselves. This can be threatening to self-harm, kill themselves, or do some other self-destructive action that is intended to provoke the victim into running back to them. A lot of the time, these types of threats are empty; they're merely another manipulative tactic the abuser uses to lure back into the toxic relationship. However, it's important to remember here that if the abuser does go through with their threat to hurt themselves, it's in no way, shape, or form your fault. You are not to blame for their actions, only they are in control of what they do, not you. Under no circumstances should you feel guilty, nor should you feel obliged to give the relationship another try. That would mean the manipulation had worked.

Undermining Your Parenting Skills/Making You Seem Like the 'Bad Guy'

Your abuser may have already undermined your parenting skills and made you out to be mean and unfair to your children whilst in the relationship, and this can continue afterwards, too. Coercive partners will take what you love and use it as a weapon against you, so using your children as a pawn in their game of manipulation is to be anticipated. It can be something as subtle and apparently innocent as not adhering to the bedtime rules, allowing your children to make their own rules up, and as such they begin to resent you when you try to implement those rules. The abuser may do as much as they can to keep the children on side; offering them expensive gifts, having a lack of discipline, letting them get away with unacceptable behavior - in some cases, poor behavior is encouraged when it will affect the abuser's victim, such as the children not listening or purposely being mean. Contradicting the rules you have in place for your children is an attempt to make you seem like the 'lesser parent', the one who is needlessly cruel and strict.

Another tactic utilized by a controlling ex-spouse is to withhold vital information about the children from you, or drip feed you important bits of information to keep you in a heightened state of anxiety. The abuser would relish in the fact that you need them in order to obtain the information you're seeking, and as such, extracting those details from the abuser is often far from easy.

Discrediting you as a parent rarely stops at just your children; that's seldom enough to make the abuser feel the dominance he needs. The lies and insertions that come out of an abusive ex's mouth can often be hurtful and shocking, so remember this should you come to hear any vile, venomous lies being told about you to peers and family. From being a drug-addict, to having numerous affairs, to not wanting your children... the malicious lies and slurs about your liability as a mother can feel like a dagger to the stomach when you first hear them. In this scenario, you need to retain as much logic as you possibly can; think about *why* they're spreading these lies. Your natural instinct is often to snap back and deny those ludicrous lies, but please remember it's what the abuser wants. They want you to exasperate yourself, denying the allegations so furiously that you look guilty of the things you're being accused of.

Stopping/Withholding Monetary Support

An abusive spouse would typically still behave in ways that negatively impact their children, just to affect their victim. It's never been more true when a controlling ex refuses to pay for their children, allowing them to go without basic needs, or preventing them from being able to live in safety or comfort. I had a conversation with someone recently, and she told me how her ex refused to pay for their children unless he was with them. That meant they had to go to their dad's house for breakfast every morning, and again after school to eat. The woman was struggling to feed the children on her part-time wage, and was forced to send them off to their dad most mornings so they had food in their belly. This made the woman look 'useless' (as she put it to me) to her children, and they even commented on her lack of money and how unhappy it made them. Their dad had his own business, and it did well enough that he could pay his ex ten times more than she was entitled to in child support, but he flat out refused saying she'd spend it on herself. Money, like a lot of things to a controlling person, is there to be utilized as a weapon, a pawn, and a bargaining chip, and by withholding it, they're trying to retain the power they so desperately need.

Disregarding Children

This one is a painful one to have to step back and watch, but once the abuser has had their fill and moved on to a new partner (or victim) it's not uncommon for them to go on and start a new family and disregard the ones they already have. They may not do this as boldly as completely cutting them out of their life, but they'll slowly and coldly start by leaving your children out of their new family activities by treating them differently to their new family, or treating them as the scape-goat or black sheep of their offspring. It's heartbreaking to see this happen to your children, no matter their age. Whilst they can understand the situation more if they're older, rejected children need consoling and reassurance that they're not the problem.

When a toxic ex introduces a new partner to the children you share, it's also fairly common for them to try to make their new spouse the child's 'new' or 'other' mother, and their new partner is often pushed into the role of 'parent,' whether they or the child wants it or not. As you know, consideration of others isn't at the top of a toxic person's list of priorities.

Disrupting Your Relationship With Others

If the abuser can't have you, they certainly won't allow anyone else to have you, either. They'll go to great lengths to ensure they're not forgotten about, and can be something of a roadblock when it comes to new relationships. They can be as bold as contacting your new partner directly, to 'warn' them about you and try to scare them off. They may go as far as threatening or even physically assaulting your new partner, doing all they can to get them to run away from the relationship. If you have children, your ex may refuse to allow the children to be around your new partnership, and can try to poison your children against the idea of you moving on and being happy with someone else.

This sabotaging behavior is undeniably very stressful, particular if you find it's pushing your new spouse away from you. Feelings of helplessness, anger, frustration, and despair are difficult to overcome in this scenario, but you need to remember that this journey is a tough one and you will come out of the other side stronger. Those helpless feelings won't last forever, no matter how much you feel like they will.

"Abusers need to feel guilty about what they do."

THE LAW ON COERCIVE control differs depending on where you reside, so I do think it's a good idea to check on the stance of the law where you live. If you're in an area that is yet to recognize this type of abuse as illegal, don't take that as "you're on your own - deal with it". As I've mentioned earlier in the book, coercive control is a relatively newfound term for a very hidden form of abuse; like all things that require a change in mindset, the view on abusive behaviors will take time - but, it will happen. In some places it already has.

Chapter Eight Affirmations

=====

Every quote I've had preceding a chapter is an affirmation that resonates with me. I chose these quotes specifically because they hold a true meaning for me, and I wanted to give them to you in the hope they can resonate with you in the same way. These words helped guide me through an incredibly dark time. The source of these quotes vary; some are from other survivors to me as they helped me navigate the aftermath of leaving my ex. Others are some I thought of myself and used as fuel when I was feeling low. There's a couple here that I saw on social media, so it may not be the original quote word for word, but it's my recollection of it, and at one point in my life it bounced round my head as I healed from an abusive relationship.

"Poisonous relationships can alter our perception. You can spend years thinking you're worthless, when in reality, you're chronically underappreciated"

=====

"The only people who get upset by you having boundaries are the same people who benefit by you not having any."

"Financial abuse is a form of domestic violence"

"Confusing control with love leads you to unhappiness"

"Love is many, many things. But it's never toxic."

"The wound is the place where light enters you"

"Abusers need to feel guilty about what they do."

THANK YOU SO MUCH FOR taking the time to read this book. I hope it's been helpful, informative, and given you some food for thought at the very least. As I always like to mention, it was reading the experiences of others that helped me find the courage to leave my abusive relationship, and I hope this book can be put in that same category: to inspire change and hope.

If you've found this book to be a good resource and gained inspiration from reading it, I'd love to hear about it! You can leave a review (even include some of your own story if you would like), or head to @escapethenarcs on Instagram. We're creating a great community of survivors over there and would love to hear from you.

Here's to self compassion, self love, and empowerment.

Also by Lauren Kozlowski

Red Flags: The Dating Red Flag Checklist to Spot a Narcissist, Abuser or Manipulator Before They Hurt You
Narcissistic Ex
Malignant Narcissism: Understanding and Overcoming Malignant Narcissistic Abuse
Malignant Narcissism & Narcissistic Ex: 2-in-1 Collection
What a Narcissist Does at the End of a Relationship: Dealing With and Understanding the Aftermath of a Narcissistic Relationship
Narcissistic Rage: Understanding & Coping With Narcissistic Rage, Silent Treatment & Gaslighting
How to go No Contact With a Narcissist: How to Leave a Narcissist, Maintain No Contact & Break Free of the Toxic Cycle
Overcoming Narcissistic Abuse: A Four Book Collection to Guide You Through the Trauma and Help You Heal from Narcissistic Abuse
Trauma Bonding: Understanding and Overcoming the Traumatic Bond in a Narcissistic Relationship
Coercive Control: Breaking Free From Psychological Abuse

About the Publisher

Escape The Narcissist is about helping you find your self-worth, offering you some thought provoking ideas to change your life and aiding you in revitalizing your relationships.

With that in mind, Escape The Narcissist has one core relationship we want to focus on: the one you have with yourself.

Our website was born from a place of darkness. We've all, at some point in our lives, been on the receiving end of ill treatment from others. From being a victim of a narcissistic relationship to being mistreated by those who should protect us and not being shown the respect we deserve, these toxic relationships can affect us more than we realise.

Whilst the people behind the content of our site and books all have their own ideas and stories, they have one thing in common: they've all overcome toxicity in their lives and want to share their story.

The content of the stories, pieces of advice and actionable life changes within this site all aim to inspire, provoke a healthier way of thinking, and help to heal any negative effects you've been left with at the hands of other people.

escapethenarcissist.com

Lightning Source UK Ltd.
Milton Keynes UK
UKHW010714130322
399989UK00001B/70

9 781393 659327